Praise for *Paddock*

Mary Lou Buschi's *Paddock* is like a game of hide and seek, a primer on seeking. Structured like a play, the collection follows two girls on a quest for a mother, and a chorus narrates, empathizes, and passes judgment. "I want to go back!" says one girl but the mother "is no longer anywhere, who was once where we could go back." Surrealism, hope's "unrelenting tick," and dream are the guiding forces here. Buschi's language is spare, cryptic, beguiling, like the "Fractals in the light" the chorus names. Sexual danger and maternal longing animate these pages, urging us to "diagnose the heart."

—Catherine Barnett, author of *Human Hours, The Game of Boxes,* and *Into Perfect Spheres Such Holes Are Pierced.*

~~May Lou Buschi~~

PADDOCK

Mary Lou Buschi (signature)

LILY POETRY REVIEW BOOKS

Published by Lily Poetry Review Books
223 Winter Street
Whitman, MA 02382

https://lilypoetryreview.blog/

ISBN: 978-1-7347869-9-6

Cover Art: Michelle Butler

Contents

Three: Night

PADDOCK

Palindrome

born inside a root
every periphery a turning

thoughts forked down
below the tilling

below the possibility of light

the invisible world composed
of branches

a child's face
trace the tender lines
the idea of her set still in a high branch

*

the idea of her set still in a high branch
trace the tender lines
a child's face

of branches
the invisible world is composed

below the possibility of light
below the tilling
thoughts forked down

every periphery a turning
born inside a root

One

They Set Off

Chorus

Once, as there are many,
time stretches infinitely,
2 girls set forth,
to find a mother,
who is She,
who is I,
who is Dear.

They Set Off Again

Girl 1

There is a nest
of thistle we must pass
and a shadow gliding over us—

Girl 2

What are we waiting for?

Girl 1

Lures slipping into streams,
burrs stuck to white cotton dresses,
and the light, there is so much of it.

Girl 2

I'm tired, I need...

Girl 1

Keep moving—the wren pleas for us.

Chorus

They climbed for
nine days,

walked a hundred miles,

looking

to find

home.

Girl 2

These woods are a made-up kingdom
where girls can die
a thousand deaths
only to emerge even more beautiful.

There is a carriage in this wood
lead by Camarillos,
expressive eyes, well-defined withers
long arched necks.

We are always young in this story,
sloppy curls, lashes casting long shadows,
wind curling around us.

Girl 1

Until a metal bed is pushed into the dark.

Girl 1

Lost? No, there is a crystal storm and moss grass
where the path forks, a mountain
between two valleys where the goats graze.

I know there will be herring, chunks of bread,
a star pool that will glisten and fire,
though there is black tarn hidden
deep among the trees.

I know because one story has ended
as another began, witnessing one
or another outcome.
It's happening—
happening now.

Girl 2

We are here!

We are here!

Chorus

They find mothers everywhere,

in the purple petals that

bloom like a rash over bark,

on the soft powder washed up on glass,

in the mouth of an orchid,

that secret tongue.

Chorus

They made a paddock for goats to graze in,

built parents out of branches,
                           leaves, and bluestone.
Served dirt and water as drink,
                softened wood into chicken,

and shaped mulberry mud pies.

*

Girl 2

My father is late tonight.
           Yours might be coming up the path,

or he might be the same father,
                or someone else's father?

Girl 1

Serve the meal,

later we'll sift through the tangled path of that.

Girl 1

It's story time. There were two girls…

Girl 2

No, not this time. I'll tell it. In my story there is only one.

The mother watched him spoon cold soup into the back of a plastic truck and pretend to heat it. She'll be fine, he said. She'll eat it. But the mother couldn't leave well enough. She poured the wet noodles into a pot, lit the blue flame and carried the girl's body into her lap. I told you she is yours, he said. But she doesn't look anything like me, she said. She has thick black bangs, and a sullen face. She looks like you. Yes, he said, I did that to hurt you.

Girl 1

What are you doing?

Girl 2

Assembling a box of toys—

Girl 1

But your box is round,

and full of fluid,

full of whispers and black channels,

a blue-eyed doll,

a grey cat, and a speckled sparrow.

Girl 2

Yes, I want to make whole, of these fragments.

If only to invite her in.

Chorus

Restless girls feeding their goats.

The oldest Wether looking down
                    on them. The other
below on a sharp turn,
                    hind facing.
The third left long ago.
If space is flat then it must start repeating.
Look long enough and there are two more girls,
far more goats.

Girl 2

Mangy old goats, I'm tired of them

and of this mist,
                    this green sky.

Girl 1

Then you be the big sister. I'm done with always telling you to

sweep the dirt into a table.

Wipe your face

and stop asking so many questions.

We are only light.

We have no voice.

Our skirts are made of smoke,

our eyes, concentric circles.

You don't listen!

Girl 2

It's you who doesn't hear.

Daughter Universes I.

The baby must be fresh,
the eye a hall of mirrors.
Stuff the mouth full of wanting.
Gently lower your baby into the ink.
Sink the silhouette into an undulating field.

A small black shape approaches,
strange rhythm.

Try to imagine building a particular world
for such a shape.

I never planned on capturing you.

Follow the lines on paper.
Affix the baby onto a wooden block.
You could print thousands of babies,

miles and miles of babies—

You were my first work
before going home,
before the dance had ended.

Girl 1

The season will change soon.
The wind will gust and the light will be low.

Girl 2

Where will we be by then?

Girl 1

Somewhere between the Toad Lily and the Aster.

We have been traveling long
in this light,

but someday it will be dark
and there will be nowhere to step,
if only to float.

Girl 2

Did you hear that?

      Voices echoing in the woods.

Girl 1

What are they saying?

Girl 2

      Whisperings words; gestures of caution?

Twilight

He was in the brook,
          pants down-round his ankles.
He had a gun, a knife,
          a love-note sealed with a wax drop.

They did what any young girls would,
          laughed, thought him ridiculous,
his sagging parts, desperately white and vulnerable
          when, he took one giant step—
They ran over slick shale and loose slag.

A family barbeque,
          a din through the long column
of trees. They could hear his beating breath,
          the rise and slap of his gait.

Girls tossing rancid petals—
          The sky complicit, blue eye won't shut.

The path grew light at the opening, a winged
          thing stretched. Snickering beautifuls
running from the sex that may one day gag
          them with its black feathers.

Girl 2

I dreamed we were traveling on our path

where marigolds meet the sky.

The sky narrowed and light grew grey.

Then you were gone.

I think that is death?

Girl 1

Waking as flesh,

that is death.

Chorus

Squirrels quick
over a thin wire.

Bird following bird—

footprints pressing
down the Yarrow Nettle.

When the Nettle springs up,
the girls will be gone.

Chorus

At last, the forest grew quiet

                                                          to the edge of the
    ravine.

Two

Dear _____,

Girl 2

Dear _____,

If you thread the branches in your sightline

what could you make?

Constellation of what?

On clear nights, we see the head of a goat,
and the body of a fish.

On those same nights,

the chokecherry whispers,

Amalthea, Amalthea.

Daughter Universes II.

Soft clay cannot be attached to hard clay
the way thoughts cannot be attached
to the darkening shadows of trees
at the close of day.

We all grow old, the shrinking and flattening
of clay particles water leaves during drying.
Even dead wood flakes and splinters,
exposed to perpetual rain, snow heft, and
streaming rays. It's here I say, I love you.

Clay pieces must be no thicker than 1 inch unless
they are hollow, and if hollow spaces are enclosed,
a pinhole must be made in the piece to allow gases
and trapped air to escape.

Bones are hollow,
carry blood, shrink, and collapse.
Thicker pieces should be allowed to dry
thoroughly before firing.

Dry limbs slowly, away from temperature extremes,
to prevent uneven drying, shrinkage, and cracking.
This is especially true of pieces, which have been joined,
such as hands, hips, eye-socket, cheeks-to-chin.

Avoid stress—unnatural bending or forcing
will cause particles to become unaligned,
resulting in chasms that will never be scarred
with enough tissue to bridge the gap.

Clay must be wedged to ensure proper alignment
to create uniform texture, and most importantly,
to drive air between the infinitesimal distance between us.

Girl 2

Let's play a game: mother in a blanket, stiff as a board.

Hold her in your arms, then slide her out to your fingers.

Girl 1

She is looking ill.

Girl 2

She's looking worse.

Girl 1

She is dying.

Girl 2

She is dead.
*
Chorus

           The girls withdraw their fingers,

       tiny snapped twigs.

The mother held there,

                     little ash

cloud

      no breath, no heartbeat.
*

Girl 2

Her death   painless,
                   like a liquid skating down her throat.

Girl 1

She went quick,
                   without sentiment.
*

Chorus

No one wintering here.

                   No one waiting to be born.

Chorus

She dreams a walnut tree bending toward a Magnolia, drifting shadows from leaves flipping in the light. Girls running through blues and greys. A canvas, the size of the sun. It's early summer, the breeze sweet when, leaves start to fall, until the canvas is covered, until the canvas is lost, and the sky is a dry socket. She begins raking leaves until there is snow. She rakes them into snow, rakes them into starlings, into the sounds of darkening.

Waking is lifting stones from your chest.
One thousand one, one thousand two, repeat.

Girl 2

Dear _____,

We saw you painting a chair.

You look reckless.

We want to meet you.

She

had a doll with a knob
at the back of its neck.
The doll had three expressions: happy, hysterical,
and one she couldn't figure.

She wanted to test the spirit realm.
Turned the doll's face to happy.
Left her in the woods.

In the morning—happy.

The next night
turned her face to hysterical,
covered her with a woolen cloth.

In the morning—hysterical.

The last night,
the expression she couldn't figure.

Put her in back of the closet,
kept an eye on her all night,
dared the spirits but
by morning, that same face.

Girl 2

Tell me again about the doll factory
where you saw melting cheeks,

unblinking eyes of violet and coal.
Where there were hundreds of spiked skulls,

empty shoulder rims, fat outstretched
hands, solid lungs beneath

a sheet of soft plastic the texture of nectarine;
knees that don't bend,

heads turning a full circumference.
While the others are fully formed

resting in cellophane nests,
out of the empty casts,

out of the metal press,
throats that will never close

resulting in a beautiful death:
chocking on a foreign substance turned to pearl.

Girl 1

Dear _____,

    The unrest of the ocean in February

frothing from its cracked mouth,

    reaching from the pit of itself,

is beating out the sound of hunger.

    Listen hard enough,

O' these paths galactic,

    O this hour that billowed, you will hear us.

Girl 2

Wishing is like a stone around my neck,

yet it's deep inside me…

Girl 2

Fine to make a game of it,
        to make a shape of it.

At night we
        carve mothers out of black sky.

Then we swim in her,

        fly in her,

        open our eyes wide in her.

Girl 1

The bride wore Italian lace
sewn into interlocked stars.

Each night she entered through the bedroom window,
six flights up, glided like an exhale into the kitchen
and jumped to her death.

Girl 2

No, not jumped, pushed. She was pushed.
Tell the story right.

Girl 1

The earthborn children suffered for it: sweats, fever,
blue limbs weighing into water,
as the mother washed them down.

The children slept foot to cheek in a single bed,
while the mother sat upright, night after night,
skin so pallid as she kept watch.

Girl 2

But the mother meant to fix it all back.
She packed the bedclothes, closed the shades,
smoothed their hair, tied their shoes,
put her arms around them,
to diagnose the heart—
Unrelenting tick: Hope. Hope. Hope.

Bloody Mary

Mother of blood and flesh
      we said your name 3 times,
walked backward up the stairs,
      then followed you to the weed choked creek
where the bluegills suck the air,
      taught you to mine for clay,
to mold bowl after bowl,
      taught you the word, ashtray
Mouth upon mouth—

Now with a spool of yarn twisted
      around your slim fingers
you want us to weave our fingers
      into your cradle.

Mary you are just a plain girl,
      a hollow grin, sloping shoulders,
hair hanging in matted nests.
      It's been a long time since you first lived.
A fish jumping out of a still creek.

Chorus

The girls traveled through forests filled with bramble that caught on their hair and sliced small nicks on their arms and cheeks / until the sea / where they coaxed her into bewilderment / She walked to the edge of the tide / watching seafoam pop / when the girls rushed out a wave / She tried to catch the small breath paths / down into that wild pit of fear where there is no sight.

Girl 1

Dear _____,

    You made it back to the ocean.

The small prints are from us.

I'm writing to tell you,

          the sea is trying to greet you.

That is what all this weather is about.

    Take a walk.

        Let the waves roll you in.

Chorus

She sees a ruined strand,

        two moving shapes.

To add up all the possible ways

        in which this present arrived,

two girls, two hidden realities,

        while she sifts through dirty sand,

lifts bits of colorful glass,

        pounded smooth by the surf,

puts them in her pockets.

        Later, she will wash them, dry them.

Fractals in the light.

Girl 1

It's time to practice.

Lie still without giggling.

Girl 2

I don't know what dead is?

Three

Night

Night Swimming

She has a thick rope of skin
where the flesh was sewn back together
after a metal fence scored and pulled
her thigh apart. She was 15, running
away from a man with a rifle,
swimming her way home.

She jumped
without knowing how deep or far
the bushes would fall.
The air sucked out through the shell
of her lungs; what was up, what was down.
He held the gun on his hip, "Come out or I'll shoot."

All but one flying through manicured shrubs,
one who sat shivering, told to disrobe, told
the police will come, as an orange veil of light
slid slowly up the drive.

It was a gaping hole, big enough for a fist.
In the dark it looked like a purple bruise,
so deep it wasn't bleeding
until she started to run.

Her father watched the surgeon
examining the sides of the laceration
for a gate of skin to pull and sew shut.

Her thigh tight for years, a yard missing,
a chasm she'd never discuss, while he,
the one who didn't make it,
turns up the drive, climbs the stairs,
to dive inside the furious oscillation
of her bedroom fan, both of them cut to ribbons.

Girl 2

I want to go back!

Girl 1

But where? Since she is no longer anywhere,
who was once where we could go back.

Ride

When he slapped her
      she held the hot blow on her cheek
and continued to love him.

They rode bikes.
      She still had training wheels,
not permitted to leave the drive,
      so, she'd make hard circles,
leaning into the center
      until he dared her to ride away.

She went to his house without her bike.
      He came around the side,
on his Schwinn, told her to climb on,
      he'd show her what balance felt like.
She didn't know where to put her hands.

The air thick, her throat dry, as the rush
      came up over the slate, up-rimmed from
thick roots; a catalog of house sailing past.

Her father standing in the drive under
      the shadow of the open door,

turns to leave her, in the garage
      among the boxes of forgotten things.

Girl 2

Little mother,

where

are you going?

She

shook a Magic Eight Ball

        asked

                if

she will marry—

                if she will carry—

But when she asked for names,

           it answered, yes
                  no and no

then

           yes

           yes

           yes

Chorus

At this tremendous depth,

there is no

sunlight.

Girl 2

Dear _____,

I am sorry you think you are imagining this.

Open your eyes.

The sunrise is a lucid stain.

One morning we meet. One morning we don't.

There is nothing to be undone.

Chorus

Have you ever been in a small ocean,
seen familiar white stars
hidden deep around long banks of coral?

Snow crabs and sea urchins huddle on all sides.
Over the water, thin shadows twitch and glide.

There is another ocean growing inside that small ocean,
full of silence, brown cotton-grass, sopped
with white foam.

On the strand beside the toss
and stretch of each cast off wave
a small goat obediently waits.

Told to do this, by what, by whom?
His waiting keeps the oceans apart.

Have you ever seen the small ocean inside the other ocean?
White stars, coral banks thick with crabs, sea urchin,
shadows twitching past.

On the strand, the goat—
Waves turning over. And the goat, the goat,
the goat, carried away.

Chorus

Watching waves plumb the sand,

        image of want.

           The woman unravels a mistake—

    dropped stitch.

She watches her friend carry

        the dead child for a week—told it's better this way

and then the after,   every   day from then.

Some say it could have been an anxious bird lodged in her throat,

           or a colony

of red ants coursing

        through her veins;

      She said it was an air raid siren letting loose,

a hollow bowl of crowing.

Girl 1

Let us go then.

Girl 2

Without light?

Girl 1

What is there to see?

Mammary Duct Ectasia

She told her friend that she knew how hard it was—

kite of knives pushing through

                lactiferous ducts,

but she doesn't.

Nothing has ever left her body

                with that much force. Nothing inside her

wringing to get out.

Girl 2

Dear _____,

I see you have packed your things.
Could this mean an ending?

I was told that endings signify grief.
Grief is a funny word, so much energy in the "grrrrr"

only to exhale every ounce of breath, ieeeef"
To be breathless is to die, I think?

Did you hear the wind hitting the shells
you've hung, or see the blue light

bending through butterfly wings?
Feel the sticky dust on the stamen from lilies?

we were there,

and there and there.

Girl 2

We are lost. Which way?

Girl 1

Way? We haven't moved an inch

in all of our lives.

Girl 2

How many have there been?

Girl 1

Lives?

One.

Many.

None.

Chorus

Into the molar

                a tongue.

Into a neckline,

             the body leaps.

Through sleeves go   two arms.

         Into the sky

Pigeons   tossed.

Into the door of her heart

                    an echo of foxglove.

Into a sock   goes the foot.

Into the wind

                       twine unraveled

          to its wooden reel.

Chorus

There again they go

into the deepest, cellar.

Sky

Vaporous mirror; vapid eye—
What is it that you want from me,

tip the earth—shake it dry?
Out of its pockets what will fall?

Lost sock, earring back, pet bones,
Dead skin, dead I, dead roots between your teeth.

What do you need to catch with your hook and line—your
    seine of stars?

All of us swaying—

Good night—Good night.

Girl 1

Dear _____,

Today our world is drenched.
We wrap ourselves in blues.
It's always cold in our world
so we sleep under the bellies of our goats,
when they are goats. We lose track of them
and what they become.

You have been trying to love us into your world,
starfish swimming in and out of you.

This will be my last letter.
Our story sketches where we've been,
where we will be,
no matter when you read this letter—
When you never read this letter.

Chorus

A ribbon slipped.
A sheet snapped smooth

then released.

The body as if loosening—

Girl 1

It's done.

Girl 2

How can you be sure?

Girl 1

She stopped thinking of us.

Girl 2

Maybe it's just begun?

Notes

Pg. 12 The Line "tangled path of that" from "They made a paddock for the goats to graze in" owes tribute to Laura Kasischke.

Pg. 25, Amalthea refers to the foster mother of Zeus who sometimes appeared as a goat.

Pg. 26 Daughter Universes II. uses found lines from an instructional guide on firing pottery.

Pg. 33 "O' these paths galactic, / O this hour that billowed" quotes Paul Celan, from "So Many Constellations," translated by Pierre Joris.

Pg. 34 Owes tribute to Roland Barthes, March 24, 1978 entry in *Mourning Diary* translated by Richard Howard.

Pg. 37 Bloody Mary is a game played by children, usually to conjure the spirit of Bloody Mary said to reveal the future.

Pg. 44 Owes tribute to Roland Barthes, August 1, 1978 entry in *Mourning Diary* translated by Richard Howard.

Pg. 52 "Let us go then" owes tribute to Waiting for Godot, Samuel Beckett.

Acknowledgements

I am grateful to the editors of the following publications where these poems first appeared, sometimes in different form.

Field, "Ukiyo-e"
Thrush, "They set off again," "I'm assembling a box of toys"
Radar, "The Goat"
Ping Pong, "Sky"
Stirring, "Night Swimming"
Indolent Beast, "Ride"
Dodging the Rain, "The bride; wore Italian lace," "Let's play
     a game," "The girls traveled
     through forests," "I've lost sight of the way"
Menacing Hedge, "Doll," "There were three," "They find
     mothers everywhere"
Dream Pop, "Twilight"
Softblow, "Into the Molar"
Pretty Owl Poetry, "Doll Factory"
Cleaver, "Bloody Mary"
SWWIM Everyday, "Mammary Duct"
Yellow Chair, "Firing"
Anderbo, "Palindrome"
Stone Highway Review, "They made a paddock for the goats
     to graze in"
Vector, "The forest is dark, the road dangerous," "It's Time
     to Practice"
Hermeneutic Chaos, "They will come and take away the snakes
     and frogs"

Some of these poems in various forms appeared in a chapbook:
     Ukiyo-e, published by Dancing Girl Press, 2014.

"Fine to make a game of it" was included in an anthology,
     Mother is a Verb.

Thank you to the many friends who read first drafts of these poems and to those who helped me to see the larger picture, in particular Rebecca Barry, Rachel Jamison Webster, and Jeff Butler. Thank you to Michelle Butler who dropped everything to read these poems and let them enter her in order to create the intoxicating painting that is now the cover. Thank you to Jackson Raisbeck for the title. Thank you to Joan Houlihan who created the Colrain Conference which was a space to explore the possibilities of, *Paddock*. I am also grateful to Patrick Donnelly, Lesley Jenike, and Catherine Barnett for their time, generous thoughts on these poems, and for their gorgeous work. Finally, thank you, most of all, Eileen Cleary and Lily Poetry Review Books for giving this book a home.

ABOUT THE AUTHOR

Mary Lou holds an MFA in poetry from the MFA Program for Writers at Warren Wilson College and a Master of Science in Urban Education from Mercy College. Her poems have appeared in many literary journals such as *FIELD, Willow Springs, Indiana Review, Radar, Thrush, Tar River, Cream City, Pank, Rhino, The Laurel Review,* among others. Mary Lou is the author of one earlier collection of poems, *Awful Baby.* She is also the author of three chapbooks. Mary Lou has received fellowships from The Santa Fe Writer's Conference, Vermont Studio Center, and The New York City Teaching Fellows. Currently, she is a special education teacher in the Bronx.

CPSIA information can be obtained
at www.ICGtesting.com
Printed in the USA
JSHW050748010621
15333JS00003B/126